A  'SPACE

Written by Brian Jones
Illustrated by Peter Rutherford

© 1992 Henderson Publishing Limited

Henderson Publishing
Woodbridge, England

OUR BACKYARD IN SPACE

The Solar System
The Earth is one of nine planets orbiting the Sun. The planets have no light of their own and only shine by reflecting sunlight. They appear as bright, starlike objects when seen in the sky. Most can be seen with the naked eye although you need binoculars or a telescope to see the three outer planets.

There are lots of other objects in the Solar System including the asteroids, comets and meteoroids.

Spinning Worlds
The planets are all spherical and all spin round. The time it takes for a planet to spin once is called its *day*. Venus spins very slowly. A day there is equal to 243 Earth-days! Jupiter spins very quickly in just under 11 hours.

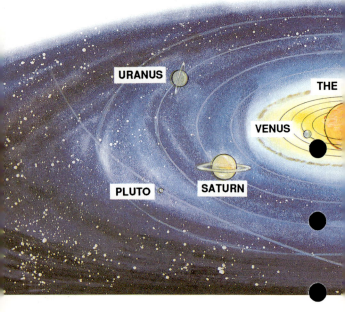

Planetary Orbits

The planets travel around the sun in paths which are almost circular. These paths are called *orbits*. Innermost Mercury orbits the Sun in just 88 days while distant Pluto takes 248 years to travel once around the Sun! The time it takes for a planet to orbit the Sun is called its *year*.

As the planets orbit the Sun they seem to move through the sky against the starry background. The word "planet" comes from an old word meaning "wandering star".

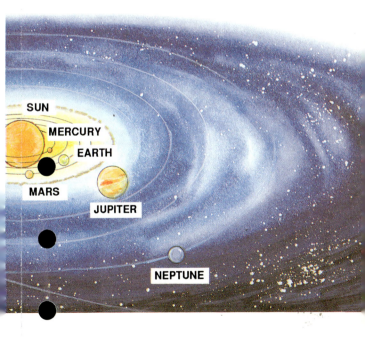

THE SUN

The Sun is a star and only appears so much brighter than the other stars because it is so much closer. Many stars are bigger and brighter than the Sun and only seem fainter because of their huge distances.

Making Sunshine
The Sun is a huge ball of hot gas 1,392 million kilometres in diameter and is made up mainly of a gas called hydrogen. The temperature at the Sun's core is a whopping 15,000,000°C and the pressure is many thousands of times the air pressure at the Earth's surface. The Sun creates energy at its core by squashing atoms of hydrogen together to form another gas we call helium. Energy is formed which slowly makes its way to the surface from where it escapes as light and heat. The Sun has been shining for about 5,000 million years and will carry on shining for as long again before its supply of hydrogen runs out.

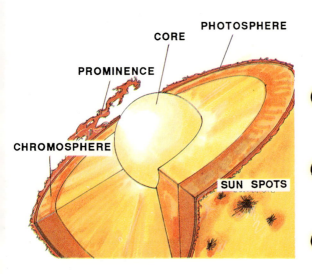

The Active Sun

The yellow surface of the Sun is called the photosphere. Here, the temperature is 5,500°C. Many different features are visible on or above the photosphere. These include sunspots, areas which are cooler than the surrounding photosphere and which appear as dark patches. Huge streamers or arches of hot gas, called flares and prominences, sometimes leap up from the Sun's surface.

Warning

NEVER look directly at the Sun with the naked eye or your eyes could easily become damaged. Also, NEVER look at the Sun with binoculars or a telescope or you may be permanently blinded.

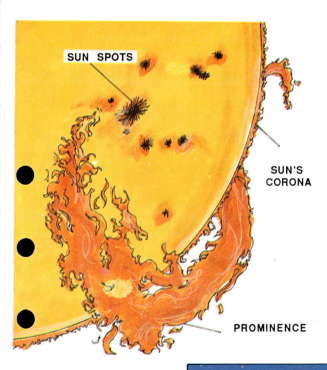

THE HOT PLANETS

Mercury
Mercury is the closest planet to the Sun. It orbits the Sun every 88 days at a distance of 58 million kilometres. Its diameter is only 4,880 kilometres. There is no atmosphere and the surface temperature can reach 350°C during the day and drop to −170°C at night.

A Cratered World
Mercury always appears close to the Sun in the sky and is difficult to see from Earth because of the Sun's glare. Our first really good views of the planet came from the American Mariner 10 spacecraft. This flew past the planet three times in 1974 and 1975 and showed a world pitted with craters, rather like the Moon.

Venus

With a diameter of 12,100 kilometres Venus is nearly as large as Earth. It is the second planet out from the Sun which it orbits once every 225 days at a distance of 108 million kilometres.

Poisonous Clouds

Venus is the brightest planet and is often seen either in the east before sunrise or in the west after sunset. Dense white clouds which completely cover the planet reflect sunlight very well.

Underneath the clouds is a poisonous atmosphere nearly 100 times as thick as Earth's. Made up mainly of carbon dioxide, this traps the Sun's heat giving surface temperatures as high as 480°C.

Surface Features

Space probes have shown craters and volcanoes, huge mountains and deep valleys on Venus. The highest mountain, called Maxwell Montes, towers 11 kilometres above the Venusian surface.

EARTH: OUR HOME

The Earth is the third planet out from the Sun. It orbits the Sun once every 365¼ days at a distance of about 150 million kilometres. The Earth was formed around 4,500 billion years ago, at the same time as the other planets. This makes the Earth and the rest of the Solar System very old indeed!

Life on Earth

Life began to appear after around a billion years. Over time, it has evolved to suit the temperature and other conditions on our planet.

The Earth is at just the right distance from the Sun to make it not too hot and not too cold for life. There is also a great deal of water on our planet. Water is very important for life. The atmosphere is also ideal for us.

Day and Night

The Earth spins once every 24 hours and it is this spinning that causes day and night. Daytime occurs on the side of the Earth facing the Sun and night on the side of the Earth facing away.

See for Yourself

You can see what happens if you stand in a darkened room with an Earth globe. Now shine a torch on the globe to represent sunlight. By spinning the globe you will see how different parts of the Earth are carried into and out of the sunlight.

A Divided Earth!

The Earth is divided into two halves which we call hemispheres. These are separated by an imaginary line running right round the Earth. This is the *equator*. It divides the northern and southern hemispheres. The Earth spins on an imaginary line, called the Earth's *axis*, which runs through the north and south poles.

The Leaning Earth

The Earth is tilted in space. It always leans the same way which means that as it travels along its orbit the northern and southern hemispheres point alternately towards the Sun. This is the main cause of the seasons.

The Seasons

In June, when the northern hemisphere is tilted towards the Sun, it gets more sunlight. The Sun climbs higher in the sky during the day in summer than in winter. The days are longer and the nights shorter. It is summer in the northern hemisphere. The southern hemisphere is tilted away from the Sun and so gets less sunlight. It is winter in the southern hemisphere. The days are shorter and the nights longer.

When it is summer in one hemisphere it is winter in the other. When neither hemisphere is tilted towards the Sun, in March and September, days and nights are the same length anywhere on the Earth. It is then when spring and autumn occur.

THE MOON

The Moon is the Earth's only natural satellite and is the closest object to us. It is 3,476 kilometres across, over a quarter of the size of Earth. The Moon is the only other object in the sky that people have landed on. Astronauts first reached the Moon's surface on the American Apollo 11 spacecraft in July, 1969.

Lunar Phases

The Moon seems to change shape from night to night. It doesn't really change shape at all. Half the Moon is lit up by the Sun at any one time and the shape, or *phase*, depends on how much of the lit half is facing us. We can't see a New Moon because the lit half is turned away from us. As the Moon orbits the Earth different amounts of the bright side face us and we see a crescent or a Half Moon. A Full Moon is seen when the whole of the lit half is facing Earth.

The Moon's Orbit

Lunar Phases

How the Moon was Formed

The Moon was formed many millions of years ago when a small planet collided with the Earth and parts of the object were thrown into orbit around our planet. These chunks came together to form the Moon.

Surface Features

The Moon's surface has light and dark areas. The light areas are cratered regions. If you look at the Moon through binoculars or a small telescope you will see lots of craters. These were formed as chunks of rock, called **meteorites**, crashed into the Moon long ago. The dark areas are called seas because astronomers of long ago used to think that there was water on the Moon.

THE RED PLANET

Nearly the whole surface of Mars is dry, reddish desert. This colour is very prominent from Earth and Mars looks just like a bright, red star. This is why it is called the Red Planet. Mars is a rocky world about half the diameter of Earth but larger than the Moon.

A Dry World

Mars has a very thin atmosphere made up mainly of carbon dioxide. There is very little oxygen or water vapour in the Martian atmosphere although Mars does have two polar ice caps. Thin clouds can also be seen above the Martian surface.

Space Missions to Mars

Lots of space probes have visited Mars. Most of these have either flown past the planet or gone into orbit around it, but in 1976 the two American Viking probes landed on the surface. They carried out many experiments and searched for signs of life, although they didn't find any! Pictures taken by space probes have allowed scientists to map the whole of the Martian surface.

Surface Features

Mars has many craters, mountains and valleys. There is a huge volcano called Olympus Mons which is 25 kilometres high and about 500 kilometres across! There is also a gigantic valley called Vallis Marineris stretching around 4,000 kilometres across the Martian surface. These features are larger than any found on Earth.

Martian Moons

Mars has two moons called Phobos and Deimos.

THE ASTEROIDS

Tiny Worlds

In between the orbits of Mars and Jupiter there are thousands of tiny objects. These are the asteroids. Most are found in the Asteroid Belt although some travel well away from this region. The asteroid Icarus travels even closer to the Sun than Mercury! The largest asteroid is Ceres. Its diameter is only 930 kilometres, making it much smaller even than our Moon. Only one asteroid, Vesta, is ever visible to the naked eye. The rest are all quite faint. They can only be seen with telescopes or binoculars and they look just like faint stars. The word "asteroid" actually means "starlike".

What are Asteroids?
The asteroids may be material left over from when the Solar System was formed, and may be bits of matter which never collected together to form a planet.

Unusual Shapes
Most asteroids are irregular in shape. A famous example is Eros. Eros has been found to be cigar-shaped!

Naming Asteroids
An asteroid is given a name only after its orbit has been worked out and so far only 3,000 or so have been named. Some asteroids have unusual names, like Petunia, which was named after a flower!

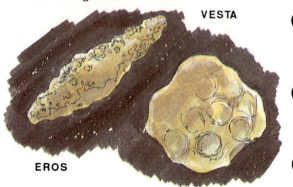

VESTA

EROS

GIANT PLANETS

Jupiter and Saturn are the two largest planets and are made up mainly of gas. Both planets have rocky central cores. Jupiter is immense with a diameter of 142,800 kilometres. If hollowed out, 1,300 Earths could fit inside! Saturn is almost as big and measures 120,000 kilometres across. Views of Jupiter and Saturn show only the tops of their deep atmospheres. There are cloud layers which appear as light and dark bands. Jupiter's clouds are much more impressive than those of Saturn. Jupiter has 16 moons and Saturn has 18! One of Jupiter's moon is called Io. Cameras on the American Voyager 1 and 2 spacecraft showed lots of volcanoes erupting on its surface.

Saturn
Orbiting the Sun at a distance of over 1,400 million kilometres, Saturn is nearly twice as far away as Jupiter. It takes nearly 30 years to make a single orbit!

Saturn's Rings
When seen through even a small telescope Saturn is an impressive sight. Its beauty is due mainly to the wonderful system of rings which circle the planet. These rings are made up of millions of tiny icy particles.

Jupiter

Jupiter lies 778 million kilometres away from the Sun and takes just under 12 years to complete a single orbit.

The Great Red Spot

An interesting feature of Jupiter is the Great Red Spot. First seen in 1665 this huge oval feature is thought to be a vast storm.

It changes in size and can reach a length of 40,000 kilometres, over three times the diameter of Earth!

FROZEN WORLDS

The three outer planets — Uranus, Neptune and Pluto — are all very faint and invisible to the naked eye. Until recently we knew very little about them but this has all changed. In 1986 the American Voyager 2 space probe passed Uranus. It went on to fly past Neptune in 1989.

Uranus

Uranus is a gaseous planet and lies 2,870 million kilometres from the Sun, over twice as far away as Saturn! Uranus takes 84 years to make one journey around the Sun. It has a very faint ring system and a family of 15 moons. Most of these were discovered by Voyager 2.

Pluto

This icy world is only 2,400 kilometres across and orbits the Sun once every 248 years at the huge distance of 5,900 million kilometres.

Pluto's orbit takes it inside the orbit of Neptune. This happened in 1979 and until 1999 Neptune will be the outermost planet. Pluto's only moon, Charon, is about half the size of Pluto.

Neptune

Another gas planet, Neptune orbits the Sun at a distance of 4,500 million kilometres and takes 165 years to complete one orbit! Neptune has a very faint ring system, which was discovered by Voyager 2. The Voyager 2 cameras also discovered six of Neptune's eight moons.

NEPTUNE

PLUTO

COMETS AND METEORS

As well as the planets and their moons, the Solar System contains lots of much smaller objects. These include comets. A comet is like a large dirty snowball. It is made up of a frozen mixture of ice, dust and gas.

Most comets have very long orbits and for most of the time are a long way from the Sun. When they get closer the heat from the Sun melts the ice in the comet. Dust and gas then form a cloud around the comet. The bit at the centre of this cloud is called the **nucleus** and the cloud is called the **coma**. Dust and gas then escape into space to form tails. Many comets appear regularly. The most famous is Halley's Comet. This reappears every 76 years or so.

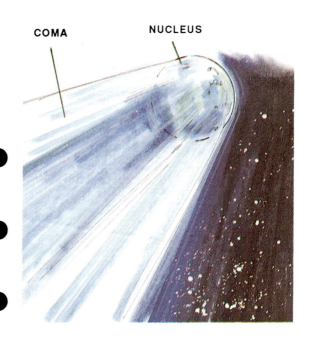

COMA NUCLEUS

Shooting Stars

There are lots of bits of dust and rock scattered through the Solar System. These are **meteoroids**. Some of these are bits that come from comets.

When tiny meteoroids enter the Earth's atmosphere, friction with air particles burns them up. We then see a streak of light in the sky. We call these streaks **meteors**, or shooting stars.

Space Rocks

Some meteoroids are so big that when they hit a planet or moon they don't burn up properly. They hit the surface and make a crater. We call these **meteorites**. The Moon's craters were formed when meteorites hit its surface billions of years ago.

The Earth has been hit many times in the past. However, most of the craters have been worn away. There are still a few left though. One of these is in Arizona and is over a kilometre across.

STARS: DISTANT SUNS

Stars are huge balls of hot gas. On really clear, moonless nights the sky seems to contain millions of stars. But you can only ever see about 3,000 stars at any one time with the naked eye. Binoculars or a small telescope will show thousands more. Some stars seem brighter than others. This may be because they are brighter, or it may be that those which seem fainter are much further away. The Sun seems so bright because it is so close. Many other stars are actually much brighter than the Sun.

Light Years

The stars are all at huge distances. They are so far away that their light takes many years to reach us.

Astronomers measure the distances to the stars and other objects in space in *light years*. A light year is the distance a ray of light travels in a year. Light moves very quickly — over a million kilometres every *four seconds*! Imagine the length of a light year!

SPACE 23

PATTERNS OF STARS

If you look closely at the night sky, some stars seem to form patterns. We call these patterns *constellations*. Many constellations used today were first named thousands of years ago. Modern star maps contain 88 constellations. We see different ones from different parts of the Earth.

Stars in a constellation are not necessarily close to each other in space. They only appear close because they lie in the same direction as seen from Earth.

The Plough
The seven stars forming the Plough are the brightest in a much bigger constellation called the Great Bear. However, the rest of the Great Bear is difficult to pick out and isn't shown on this map. The Plough is always visible from the northern hemisphere whenever the sky is dark and clear. Look for it nearly overhead during spring evenings, high in the northwest in summer, low over the northern horizon in autumn and high in the northeast in winter.

Now follow a line from Merak through Dubhe and you will find the Pole Star, the brightest star in the Little Bear.

The Little Bear
The Little Bear is made up of faint stars. Its brightest star is Polaris. This is also called the Pole Star. Polaris is very important to navigators as it always lies due north in the sky.

Cassiopeia
Although Cassiopeia is only small, it is very easy to find. Follow the line from Merak and Dubhe past the Pole Star as shown here. Cassiopeia lies on the opposite side of the Pole Star to the Plough. It can be seen high in the sky during evenings in autumn and low down over the northern horizon during spring.

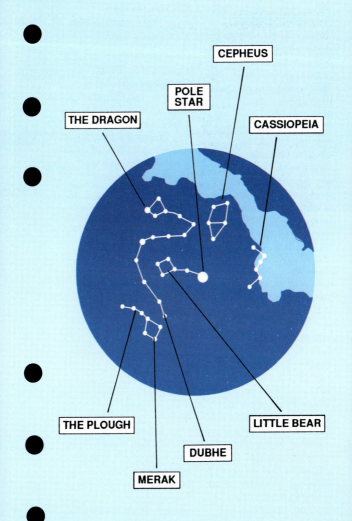

Orion

Orion is one of the most famous constellations in the sky. It represents the legendary hunter Orion and can be seen from anywhere on Earth. Those in the northern hemisphere should look in the southern sky during winter evenings. If you live below the equator you will see Orion in the northern sky during summer. Remember that when it is winter in the northern hemisphere, it is summer in the south!

Taurus

Those of you who live in the northern hemisphere will easily spot Taurus, the Bull. The brightest star in Taurus is Aldebaran. Aldebaran marks the Eye of the Bull and is found by following the line made by the three stars in Orion's Belt northwards. Aldebaran seems to be a member of a V-shaped open star cluster. This cluster is called the Hyades. Aldebaran isn't really in the cluster. It actually lies halfway between Earth and the Hyades and only seems to be a member. Look at the Hyades with binoculars and you will spot lots of stars.

Now follow the line from Orion's Belt a little further and you will come to the Pleiades open cluster. You should spot six or seven stars in the Pleiades with the naked eye. Binoculars or a small telescope will show many more.

Sirius

Now follow the line of Orion's Belt to the south. You will arrive at Sirius. This is the brightest star in the sky. It is also one of the closest. It shines from a distance of just over 8 light years.

Crux

Crux is a small but very prominent constellation. The cross-shape of Crux is easily spotted. Crux is the smallest constellation in the whole sky. For stargazers in the southern hemisphere Crux is best seen during summer when it will be high in the sky near the overhead point.

Centaurus

Crux lies near the much larger constellation Centaurus, the Centaur. According to legend, a centaur was a creature with the head and upper body of a human and the legs and lower body of a horse. The two brightest stars in Centaurus, Alpha and Beta, can be seen. Alpha Centauri is the closest bright star to Earth. The closest star of all is much fainter. It is called Proxima Centauri. This star is so faint that it can't be seen without a telescope.

Proxima is actually in orbit around Alpha Centauri. Both stars lie at a distance of just over 4 light years. Part of Centaurus loops around Crux and a number of the other stars in Centaurus are also shown here.

Achernar

If you follow a line from Gamma through Acrux as shown you should arrive at the bright star Achernar. Achernar is the brightest star in the constellation Eridanus, the River. Those of you who live in the southern hemisphere will see Achernar high in the sky during winter evenings.

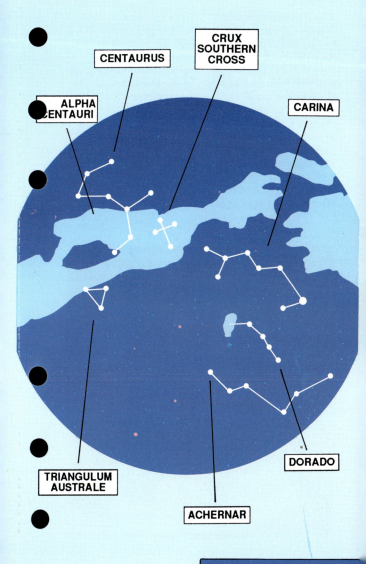

STAR CLUSTERS

Star clusters are groups of stars which stay close to each other as they travel through space. Astronomers know of well over a thousand star clusters and some of these can be seen with just the naked eye. Probably the most famous star cluster is the Pleiades (PLY-A-DEEZ) which can be seen from the northern hemisphere during winter evenings.

Another famous cluster is Omega Centauri (O-ME-GA SEN-TOE-RYE) which can be seen during autumn evenings in the southern hemisphere.

Most of the star clusters we know about are found in or around our own galaxy, although some have been found in other galaxies.

Open Clusters

There are two types of star cluster. These are **open** and **globular**. Open clusters are loose collections of stars and they don't have any real shape at all. They can have anything from just a few to hundreds of stars. The Pleiades is an open cluster. Quite often, open clusters can break up into single stars. The Sun may once have been a member of an open star cluster which broke up long ago.

Globes of Stars

As you might think from the name, globular clusters are globe-shaped. They look like huge balls of stars in space, rather like gigantic snowballs! Omega Centauri is a globular cluster. These clusters can contain many thousands of stars and are much bigger than open clusters.

GAS CLOUDS IN SPACE

The space between the stars isn't completely empty and is filled with particles of dust and gas. This is very thinly spread but in some places is much denser and forms huge clouds. Astronomers call these clouds **nebulae.**

A Star is Born

Stars are born inside nebulae. Gravity pulls particles of the dust and gas together until a ball, or **globule**, is formed. The globule gets bigger and bigger. Eventually gravity pulls it in so that it collapses and gets denser and hotter. After a time the centre of the globule gets so hot and dense that reactions start. These reactions are like those which take place at the Sun's core. Energy is given off which pushes outwards. The globule stop collapsing. It starts to give off light and heat and becomes a star. Whole nebulae form clusters of stars.

Kinds of Nebula

There are three kinds of nebula. An ***emission nebula*** contains very hot stars. These actually make the gas in the nebula shine and so it gives off its own light. The Orion Nebula is an emission nebula.

Orion Nebula

A dark nebula, like the Horsehead Nebula in Orion, contains no stars at all. These clouds are seen as dark patches against a brighter background.

Reflection nebulae don't contain any really hot stars and only reflect starlight. The dust and gas around the stars in the Pleiades open cluster form a reflection nebula.

Horseshoe Nebula

Pleiades

GALAXIES

The Milky Way Galaxy
All the stars that we see in the night sky belong to a huge spiral-shaped collection of stars we call *the Galaxy*. The Galaxy contains around 100,000 million stars as well as many star clusters and nebulae. It measures about 100,000 light years across.

Often, when the night is really dark and clear, we can see a faint misty band of light crossing the sky. This is called the *Milky Way*. Its glow is caused by the combined light from thousands of stars in our galaxy.

Shapes of Galaxies

We live in what is called a *spiral* galaxy. This resembles a huge Catherine wheel in space. There are thousands of millions of other galaxies scattered throughout the Universe. Many of these are also spirals although galaxies do come in other shapes.

Elliptical galaxies are similar in shape to rugby balls. Some galaxies look a bit like colossal globular clusters, although they contain many more stars than real globular clusters. Some galaxies are just like clouds of stars. They have no real shape and are known as *irregular* galaxies.

Other Galaxies

Our Galaxy is a member of a cluster of about 30 galaxies called the Local Group. The biggest member is the Andromeda Spiral Galaxy. This gigantic system measures 150,000 light years across and contains 300,000 million stars!

The two closest galaxies to ours are both irregular. These are the Magellanic Clouds and they can only be seen from places in the southern hemisphere.

ECLIPSES

Solar Eclipses

The Sun is much bigger than the Moon, but it is also a lot further away. Because of this, the Sun and Moon look to be about the same size in the sky.

Sometimes the Moon passes exactly between the Earth and Sun. When this happens the Moon completely covers the Sun and blocks off the Sun's light. This is called a total solar eclipse.

During a total solar eclipse the brilliant glare from the Sun's disc is cut off. It is only during total solar eclipses that the Sun's corona becomes visible.

Frightening Sights!

Total solar eclipses are impressive sights. But they can be frightening if you don't know why the Sun stops shining! Long ago, people didn't know why solar eclipses happened. Some thought the Sun was being eaten by a huge dragon! In fact, two armies who were fighting each other in 585BC were so frightened by a total solar eclipse which took place at the time that they quickly made peace with each other!

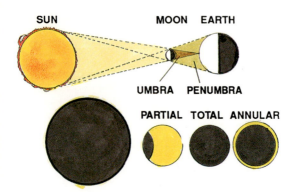

36 SPACE

Partial Eclipses

Sometimes the lining up of the Sun and Moon in the sky isn't exact. Eclipses can still happen but only part of the Sun's disc is hidden. We then see a partial solar eclipse.

Lunar Eclipses

The Moon sometimes moves into the Earth's shadow. When this happens the sunlight which was falling onto the Moon's surface is blocked off. We then see a lunar eclipse. While it is in the Earth's shadow, the surface of the Moon goes very dim and usually turns a deep coppery-red colour.

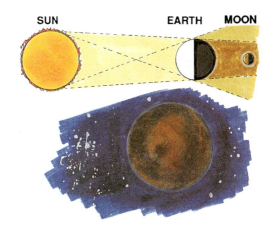

AURORAE

The Sun is giving out millions of tiny charged particles. Sometimes these can enter the Earth's atmosphere. When they do they bump into air particles. This causes certain gases in the atmosphere to glow. We call these glows *aurorae.*

Weird Shapes

Aurorae are usually seen in the sky near the north and south poles. They can have lots of different shapes. Some aurorae look like huge curtains flapping in the sky! Others look like searchlight rays reaching up from the horizon.

Aurorae are quite rare and not seen very often. If you do see one, though, it is a sight you will never forget!

ARTIFICIAL SATELLITES

Scientists have put lots of different satellites into orbit around the Earth. These are used for things such as weather forecasting, communications and for studying the Earth from orbit.

You may sometimes spot a satellite passing across the sky. When you do see one, it will look very much like a moving star. Unlike rapidly-moving meteors, a satellite may take a minute or more to cross the sky. Also, if you do think you have spotted an artificial satellite crossing the sky, make sure it isn't an aircraft. The warning lights on aircraft are usually coloured. Also, if it is a really quiet night you may hear the noise of the aircraft engines.

OBSERVATORIES

There are many large telescopes all across the Earth. Astronomers use these giant instruments to observe things which lie at colossal distances. Without huge telescopes our knowledge of the Universe would be very limited!

Observatories

The small telescopes which we might use can be carried out into the back garden when the sky is dark and clear! But the giant telescopes used by professional astronomers are far too big to move around like this. They are housed in special buildings called *observatories* which are built on high ground, such as on the top of a mountain. This is so that the telescope has to look through as little of the atmosphere as possible. The air is often dusty and murky and can spoil the view for the astronomers. An observatory site usually has a number of separate buildings, each with its own telescope. A famous one is on La Palma in the Canary Islands. Another is on Mauna Kea, one of the best sites in the world. The observatories at Mauna Kea are built on top of an extinct volcano!

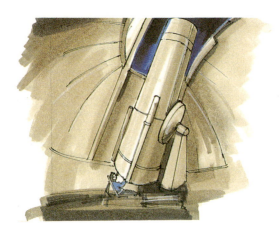

A Telescope in Orbit
Astronomers have launched a large telescope into orbit around the Earth. This is the Hubble Space Telescope, named after the famous American astronomer Edwin Hubble. With it, astronomers hope to make lots of exciting new discoveries and to look deeper into space than ever before. The Hubble Space Telescope will work better from space than from the ground because there is no atmosphere and the views will be really crisp and clear.

LOOKING AT THE SKY

Naked Eye
Many people think that you can't see anything in the sky without a telescope. This is wrong! By simply standing outside under a clear, dark moonless sky and looking up you can pick out quite a few of the constellations. The charts in this book will help you pick out some of the main ones.

Another favourite for naked eye astronomers are meteors. These are visible as streaks of light against the starry background and some can be very bright. If you lie out on a sun lounger or deck chair for half an hour or so and keep your eyes peeled, you would be unlucky not to see at least one or two meteors.

Binoculars

Binoculars will show you mountains and craters on the Moon, the four largest moons of Jupiter and quite a few star clusters and nebulae. When you're looking for star clusters, nebulae and galaxies, you do need to know exactly where to look! There are one or two of these objects shown on the charts in this book.

Telescopes

Telescopes will reveal hundreds of different objects in the night sky. They will also let you look in detail at features on the Moon's surface and on the other planets. You shouldn't really go out and buy a telescope until you have learned something about the sky. Identify some of the constellations and learn to identify the bright planets.

A good telescope can be quite expensive and so you should make sure that you get value for money. If you do buy one, try to find a shop which deals in telescopes. Many such shops advertise in astronomy magazines and can supply telescopes by post. Don't buy from department stores or general mail order catalogues as these companies don't always provide a good after-sales service.

Make a Note of it
Whenever you see anything that interests you, why not note it down? Perhaps you can have a go at drawing what you see! Don't worry if you're not a brilliant artist! Do your best and keep doing it. With practice you will get better. Why not make an observing book? You can get notebooks which have lines and blank pages facing each other. You can do the drawings you want on the blank page and describe what you see on the other.
If you do make an observing book, don't forget to make a note of the date and time that you make each entry and where you were looking from. You should also describe what telescope or binoculars you used (or whether you used any at all).

Keeping Warm

Standing outside for a long time, even on summer nights, can be quite chilly, and you should always dress properly. Thick socks and good shoes are important. If you only wear plimsolls or sandals, your feet will soon start to feel cold. You should also wear thick trousers. A good pair of jeans is ideal. A thick shirt (and a vest!) topped with a pullover and thick outer coat will keep the cold out and the warmth in. Finally, don't forget that a lot of heat from your body is lost through the head. So wear a hat or cap and a good scarf. If you go out without proper clothing, you will soon feel cold and this will spoil your enjoyment.

SPACE EXPLORATION

Before the Space Age the only way to explore the other planets was through telescopes. Now space probes have visited every planet in the Solar System apart from Pluto.

Some probes take many years to reach distant planets. Because of this scientists have to be sure that all the instruments on board will work. Each probe is tested thoroughly before launch.

Venus
Some Venus probes have actually landed on its surface and taken photographs. Some have gone into orbit and used special cameras to map the surface of Venus, even though the planet is covered in dense clouds.

Mars

The many unmanned probes that have been sent to Mars have between them sent back thousands of pictures. Scientists have been able to draw a map of the whole planet. The American Viking probes landed on Mars in 1976. They took lots of photographs of the surface and made measurements of the Martian weather. Before man landed on the Moon scientists sent unmanned probes to explore it. This helped them to pick the best landing sites and told us what it would be like when man landed there. It is important that we also explore Mars thoroughly before astronauts visit the planet. A manned mission to Mars will probably be launched by about 2015.

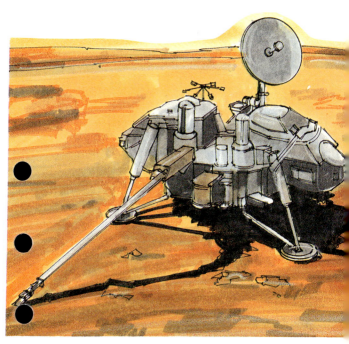

The Giant Planets

Both Jupiter and Saturn have been visited by space probes. These are the American Pioneer and Voyager probes. The cameras carried on board these craft made many discoveries including a number of new moons orbiting the planets. After visiting Saturn, Voyager 2 went on to pass Uranus and Neptune. Neptune is the furthest planet to be explored by space probe.

Comets

Halley's Comet was visited by five space probes in 1986. The best results came from the European probe Giotto which flew within a few hundred kilometres of the nucleus and sent back many interesting pictures.

The Future

Exciting space missions are being planned to other comets. One probe will actually fly with a comet as it moves along its orbit!

The Cassini mission will explore Saturn and its satellites from orbit. A special probe will be released which will hopefully give us our first view of the surface of Titan.